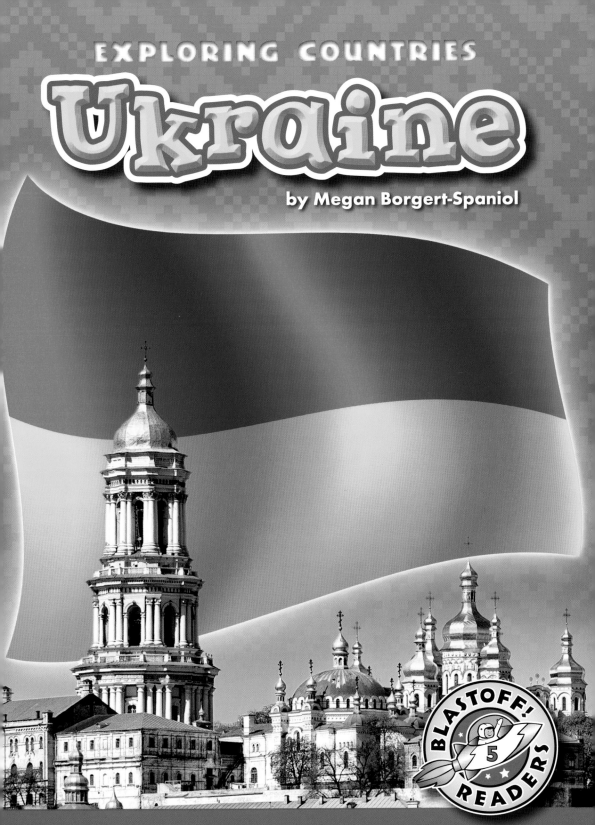

EXPLORING COUNTRIES

Ukraine

by Megan Borgert-Spaniol

BLASTOFF! READERS
5

BELLWETHER MEDIA • MINNEAPOLIS, MN

Note to Librarians, Teachers, and Parents:

Blastoff! Readers are carefully developed by literacy experts and combine standards-based content with developmentally appropriate text.

Level 1 provides the most support through repetition of high-frequency words, light text, predictable sentence patterns, and strong visual support.

Level 2 offers early readers a bit more challenge through varied simple sentences, increased text load, and less repetition of high-frequency words.

Level 3 advances early-fluent readers toward fluency through increased text and concept load, less reliance on visuals, longer sentences, and more literary language.

Level 4 builds reading stamina by providing more text per page, increased use of punctuation, greater variation in sentence patterns, and increasingly challenging vocabulary.

Level 5 encourages children to move from "learning to read" to "reading to learn" by providing even more text, varied writing styles, and less familiar topics.

Whichever book is right for your reader, Blastoff! Readers are the perfect books to build confidence and encourage a love of reading that will last a lifetime!

This edition first published in 2014 by Bellwether Media, Inc.

No part of this publication may be reproduced in whole or in part without written permission of the publisher. For information regarding permission, write to Bellwether Media, Inc., Attention: Permissions Department, 5357 Penn Avenue South, Minneapolis, MN 55419.

Library of Congress Cataloging-in-Publication Data

Borgert-Spaniol, Megan, 1989-
 Ukraine / by Megan Borgert-Spaniol.
     pages cm. – (Blastoff! Readers: Exploring Countries)
 Includes bibliographical references and index.
 Summary: "Developed by literacy experts for students in grades three through seven, this book introduces young readers to the geography and culture of Ukraine"– Provided by publisher.
 ISBN 978-1-62617-071-1 (hardcover : alk. paper)
 1. Ukraine–Juvenile literature. I. Title.
 DK508.515.B67 2014
 947.7–dc23
                                                      2013035381

Printed in the United States of America, North Mankato, MN.

Contents

Ukraine is a nation in eastern Europe. Spanning 233,032 square miles (603,550 square kilometers), it is the second largest country on the **continent**. Its capital is Kiev. This ancient city stands on the banks of the Dnieper River in the north.

Moldova and Romania are Ukraine's neighbors to the southwest. Hungary, Slovakia, and Poland line the country's western boundary. Ukraine shares part of its northern border with Belarus. Russia lies to the north and east. To the south are the Sea of Azov and the Black Sea. Their waters meet at the Kerch **Strait**.

Poland

Slovakia

Hungary

Romania

Belarus

Russia

Kiev

⭐

Ukraine

Moldova

Sea of Azov

Kerch Strait

N

W E

S

Black Sea

5

Dnieper River

Flat, **fertile** grasslands sweep across much of Ukraine. The country's major rivers flow through these plains from the northwest to the southeast. The largest is the Dnieper River. It snakes through central Ukraine before it empties into the Black Sea. Along the route, **dams** turn waterpower into electricity.

In the west, the land rises into the stunning Carpathian Mountains. This range holds Mount Hoverla, Ukraine's tallest peak. The north contains vast wetlands and forests of birch, oak, and pine. Near the southern coast, lowlands extend into the Crimean **Peninsula**. Here, the Crimean Mountains tower above the Black Sea shore.

Carpathian Mountains

The Crimean Peninsula is a unique region that juts out from southern Ukraine. It is connected to the mainland by the narrow **Isthmus** of Perekop. Saltwater **lagoons** mark the peninsula's northern coast. These shallow inlets are cut off from the Sea of Azov by the Arabat **Spit**. This thin, curved sandbar is nearly 70 miles (113 kilometers) long.

The forested Crimean Mountains march along the southern coast of Crimea. Throughout the range, streams cut through **gorges** and topple over cliffs. At the western end, rocky peaks drop sharply into the Black Sea. Farther east, they slope gently toward beaches that disappear beneath the warm waves.

fun fact

The Swallow's Nest Castle is one of the Crimean Peninsula's most famous landmarks. Perched high above the Black Sea, the castle is named after a type of bird's nest found on cliff faces.

Did you know?

Vacationers are drawn to the warm, mild climate of southern Crimea. Many visitors relax in the region's spas and resorts to improve their health.

Eurasian elk

jerboa

cormorant

The forests and marshes of northern Ukraine are home to all kinds of wildlife. Eurasian elk, wild boars, and badgers search for food among the trees. Woodpeckers fly overhead while black grouse stay hidden on the ground. Wolves, lynx, and brown bears prowl through the Carpathian Mountains. Roe deer and snow voles look out for these predators.

brown bear

Jerboas hop and marmots scurry through the grasslands of central Ukraine. Nearby rivers are filled with trout, pike, and perch. On the coast, sandpipers and black-headed gulls wade in shallow seawater. Inky black cormorants nest in groups along the rocky shore. In spring, Crimean mountain meadows come to life with bright red peonies.

fun fact

Traditional clothing called *vyshyvanka* is still popular in Ukraine today. These linen shirts are hand-stitched with colorful patterns. Long ago, the designs would differ from region to region.

Ukraine is home to around 44.5 million people. Most of them are **ethnic** Ukrainians. Russians make up the next largest group. Many have settled in Crimea along with the **native** Crimean Tatars. Belarusians, Bulgarians, and Poles are among the smaller groups that live in Ukraine. These communities often teach and do business in their own languages.

Under Soviet rule, Ukrainians were forced to speak Russian in public. The official language has since been changed to Ukrainian. Russian is still widely used, even around the capital city. Most people understand both languages. Some speak Surzhik, a combination of the two.

Speak Ukrainian!

English	Ukrainian	How to say it
hello	vitayu	vee-TIE-you
good-bye	do pobachennya	doh po-BOTCH-en-ya
yes	tak	tahk
no	ni	nee
please	proshu	PRO-shoo
thank you	dyakuyu	dee-YAH-kwee-you
friend	druk	DROOK

Most Ukrainians live in small city apartments. They ride buses, **streetcars**, and **subways** to work and school. Many also walk from place to place. They stop at cafés and small booths along the city sidewalks. In their free time, city dwellers have picnics at parks, visit museums, and go to movies or shows.

The countryside features the **traditional** *khata*, or village home. A typical khata is made of clay, logs, and straw. Colorful window frames make each home unique. Ukrainians in the countryside work on farms, tend their gardens, and do **handiwork**. They often hop on bicycles to take short trips. Buses and trains bring them into larger towns.

Where People Live in Ukraine

countryside 31.1%

cities 68.9%

! fun fact

Many city dwellers escape to summer cottages called *dachas*. They enjoy the opportunity to grow their own vegetables and breathe clean, fresh air.

Did you know?

It can be difficult for rural Ukrainians to receive a quality education. Some students must walk a long way to their school. Many also share their classroom and teacher with younger learners.

Young Ukrainians must attend school for nine years. Children begin primary school at age 6 or 7. They learn how to read, write, and do math. After four years, students move on to secondary school. During these five years, they take classes in geography, chemistry, and foreign languages. They also learn about Ukrainian literature and history.

16

After secondary school, some young people choose to work. Others go to schools that teach them specific skills. Most students continue with high school. After two years, they take a series of exams. High scores allow them to attend a university in one of Ukraine's major cities. University classes may be taught in Ukrainian, Russian, or English.

Where People Work in Ukraine

manufacturing 26%

farming 5.6%

services 68.4%

The rich soil of central Ukraine makes for some of the best farmland in Europe. Large crops of wheat, sugar beets, and sunflowers grow in this region. Potatoes thrive in the north, where cattle graze in nearby pastures. In the east, miners dig iron ore and manganese from deep in the earth. Factories use these **natural resources** to make iron and steel.

Ukraine is a major producer of heavy machinery and transportation equipment. Other **exports** include chemicals, clothing, sugar, and sunflower oil. Most Ukrainians work in schools, hospitals, and other **service jobs**. Some serve **tourists** at the spas and resorts of southern Crimea.

19

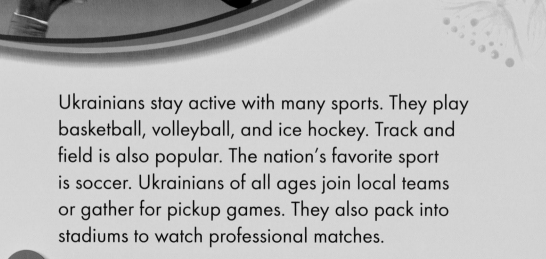

Ukrainians stay active with many sports. They play basketball, volleyball, and ice hockey. Track and field is also popular. The nation's favorite sport is soccer. Ukrainians of all ages join local teams or gather for pickup games. They also pack into stadiums to watch professional matches.

When the weather is nice, Ukrainians head outside the city to swim and hike. Many take weekend camping trips in the Carpathian Mountains. For longer vacations, families travel to the Black Sea. Coastal visitors can relax in the region's many **mineral springs** and mud baths.

Did you know?

Ukrainian folk dancers color the stage at indoor concerts and outdoor events. Their energetic kicks, twirls, and leaps attract audiences big and small.

In Ukraine, the main meal of the day takes place in the midafternoon. It often starts with *borsch*, a soup made with beets and other vegetables. Typical main dishes feature beef, pork, chicken, or fish. Rice and ground meat are rolled up in cabbage leaves for a popular side dish. Also on the side are *varenyky*. These dumplings are filled with sauerkraut, potatoes, or fruit.

Some Ukrainian dishes are linked to certain regions or holidays. *Banosh* is a traditional meal of the Carpathian Mountains. This corn porridge is topped with salty cheese, pork fat, and mushrooms. At Christmas, Ukrainians sip a drink made from dried apples, pears, and prunes. *Paska*, a sweet egg bread, has a spot on every Easter table.

fun fact

The *Pampukh* Festival in Lviv celebrates Ukraine's traditional Christmas doughnut. In 2012, the festival set a world record with a sign made out of more than 7,000 *pampukhs*!

borsch

pampukh

Ivana Kupala

Most Ukrainians celebrate the New Year before they celebrate Christmas. On New Year's Eve, children await the arrival of *Ded Moroz*, or Grandfather Frost. He leaves gifts under a fir tree. Christmas Eve takes place on January 6. Families sit down to a feast of twelve different dishes. The first is always *kutya*, a wheat porridge with raisins, nuts, and poppy seeds.

In spring, Ukrainians prepare for Easter by cleaning their homes from top to bottom. Families attend church services in the early hours of Easter Sunday. Baskets of food are blessed before the morning meal. July brings a midsummer festival called *Ivana Kupala*. Young women make wreaths out of flowers and herbs. People hold hands and jump over fires for good luck.

fun fact

A *didukh* can be found in many Ukrainian homes at Christmas. This bunch of wheat and dried flowers is a symbol of family and good fortune.

Did you know?

Pysanky symbols have changed little over time. Common designs include plants, animals, stars, crosses, and geometric shapes.

Ukraine is known for its long tradition of making decorative Easter eggs called *pysanky*. A pysanky artist uses wax to draw on an egg. When the egg is dipped in dye, the parts covered in wax are protected. This process is repeated with different colors until the design is complete. The artist melts the wax off the egg to reveal a beautiful, detailed pattern.

In the past, only women made pysanky. They would decorate the eggs with colors and symbols that represented their family or village. Specific designs were passed from mothers to daughters for centuries. Today, all members of the family make pysanky to share with loved ones. This Easter tradition brings Ukrainians closer to their rich and colorful past.

fun fact

Long ago, pysanky dyes were made with berries, roots, and tree bark. Now people use chemical dyes to achieve bold, bright colors.

Fast Facts About Ukraine

Ukraine's Flag

Ukraine's first national flag featured a yellow stripe on top and a blue stripe on the bottom. These colors were based on Lviv's coat of arms. In 1918, the colors were flipped to represent a blue sky over golden fields of wheat. Ukraine's flag changed when it was part of the Soviet Union. The blue and yellow flag was readopted in 1992 after Ukraine gained independence.

Official Name: Ukraine

Area: 233,032 square miles (603,550 square kilometers); Ukraine is the 46th largest country in the world.

Capital City:	Kiev
Important Cities:	Kharkiv, Dnipropetrovsk, Odessa, Lviv
Population:	44,573,205 (July 2013)
Official Language:	Ukrainian
National Holiday:	Independence Day (August 24)
Religions:	Christian (96.1%); Jewish (0.6%); other (3.3%)
Major Industries:	mining, manufacturing, farming, services
Natural Resources:	iron ore, manganese, coal, natural gas, oil, salt
Manufactured Products:	metals, machinery, transportation equipment, chemicals, clothing, food products
Farm Products:	grains, sugar beets, sunflower seeds, potatoes, milk, beef, poultry, pork
Unit of Money:	Hryvnia; the hryvnia is divided into 100 kopiyky.

Glossary

continent—one of the seven main land areas on Earth; the continents are Africa, Antarctica, Asia, Australia, Europe, North America, and South America.

dams—structures that block the flow of water in a river

ethnic—belonging to a group of people with a specific cultural background

exports—products that are sold by one country to another

fertile—able to support growth

gorges—deep, narrow valleys with steep, rocky sides

handiwork—work done with the hands; embroidery, pottery, and wood carving are types of handiwork.

isthmus—a narrow strip of land that connects two larger pieces of land; an isthmus lies between two bodies of water.

lagoons—shallow bodies of water protected by a barrier of sand or coral

mineral springs—natural pools of water that are rich in minerals; mineral springs are thought to have healing powers.

native—originally from a specific place

natural resources—materials that are taken from the earth and used to make products or fuel

peninsula—a section of land that extends out from a larger piece of land and is almost completely surrounded by water

service jobs—jobs that perform tasks for people or businesses

spit—a long, curved strip of sand that juts out into a body of water

strait—a narrow stretch of water that connects two larger bodies of water

streetcars—vehicles that run along tracks through city streets; streetcars are powered by electricity.

subways—underground train systems

tourists—people who travel to visit another place

traditional—relating to a custom, idea, or belief handed down from one generation to the next

To Learn More

AT THE LIBRARY

Kummer, Patricia K. *Ukraine*. New York, N.Y.: Children's Press, 2001.

Polacco, Patricia. *Rechenka's Eggs*. New York, N.Y.: Philomel Books, 1988.

Suwyn, Barbara J. *The Magic Egg and Other Tales from Ukraine*. Englewood, Colo.: Libraries Unlimited, 1997.

ON THE WEB

Learning more about Ukraine is as easy as 1, 2, 3.

1. Go to www.factsurfer.com.

2. Enter "Ukraine" into the search box.

3. Click the "Surf" button and you will see a list of related Web sites.

With factsurfer.com, finding more information is just a click away.

Index